Especially for

From

Date

Bible Memory Plan
& Devotional
for **Fathers**

Children Are an Heritage of the Lord
Psalm 127:3

GLENN HASCALL

BARBOUR BOOKS

An Imprint of Barbour Publishing, Inc.

© 2015 by Barbour Publishing, Inc.

ISBN 978-1-63058-729-1

Published by Barbour Books, an imprint of Barbour Publishing, Inc., P.O. Box 719, Uhrichsville, Ohio 44683, www.barbourbooks.com

Our mission is to publish and distribute inspirational products offering exceptional value and biblical encouragement to the masses.

Member of the
Evangelical Christian
Publishers Association

Printed in the United States of America.

Contents

Introduction

Mark Twain once said, "A man cannot be comfortable without his own approval." Twain seemed to understand that everything we attempt to be and do hinges on the roles of choice and approval. Sometimes ours—sometimes God's.

Living like Jesus often goes against our human nature. As men we can choose how we respond to our various roles in life. We may be employees, employers, uncles, husbands, friends, and dads, but each must choose how to tackle those roles.

This book takes you through biblical descriptions of dads. As men we bear a great responsibility. We must live as an example to those around us and live to influence future generations. This book will help you be an example for your kids, your family, and those around you.

For to this you have been called,
because Christ also suffered for you,
leaving you an example,
so that you might follow in his steps.
1 PETER 2:21 ESV

What we learn in the Bible provides ongoing course correction. We can't truly follow God if we've made no choice to walk with Jesus. Who are you? Why were you created? Where are you going? Is there a plan? What does a real dad look like anyway?

By committing instructions from God to memory you may be surprised just how much that choice impacts each "next step" you take.

Man

*God knew his people in advance,
and he chose them to become like his Son.*
ROMANS 8:29 NLT

The last words of sixteenth-century writer Anthony Collins were, "I have always endeavored, to the best of my ability, to serve God, my king, and my country. I go to the place God has designed for those who love him."

In just a few words Collins conveys a sense of purpose, a lifetime of duty, and a place of peace. It is easy to believe this was a man of action, allegiance, and hope.

Being a great dad means understanding who you are as a man. The role requires a sense of action and purpose. As a man you are created in the likeness of God, and you have standing orders to endure difficult circumstances.

Take the time to explore what it looks like to be a man after God's own heart. God's instructions found in the Bible shine a light in the darkness. That light informs each new step you take.

Write God's Word on Your Heart Today

This is a start on what may be a radical discovery about how God views manhood and how to relate to your children as their dad. It's a good journey, and it's affirming. . .but it may require change.

Read through the following two verses related to godly manhood. Allow your soul to be convinced that God loves you and the plan He has for you goes beyond anything you can pursue, purchase, or possess. Take the next step; memorize these verses and keep them as reminders that God's plan for you is good and perfectly designed to fit with how He made you.

God created man in His own image;
in the image of God He created him;
male and female He created them.
GENESIS 1:27 NKJV

God's holy people must endure persecution
patiently, obeying his commands and
maintaining their faith in Jesus.
REVELATION 14:12 NLT

A man of God will reflect these incredible realities in his character and his choices. The many layers of being a godly dad can start well before his first child is born, or it can be the result of "on-the-job training." So let's walk on—together.

Dear God, sometimes I'm not sure what it means to be a man. I've toyed with the idea that it means being physically strong, attractive to the opposite sex, impressive in sports, in possession of the most money, or having the nicest house in the neighborhood. Lead me to the proper meaning and right thinking of godly manhood. Amen.

Character

Come close to God, and God will come close to you. Wash your hands, you sinners; purify your hearts, for your loyalty is divided between God and the world.

JAMES 4:8 NLT

Character is how you live when there is no one around to impress. Sometimes we don't fully understand the quality of our character until we endure hard times. Ralph Waldo Emerson wrote, "What you are thunders so loudly that I cannot hear what you say to the contrary."

Each of your children have a better handle on your character than you may think. They get to see how you respond in the relative safety of your home. And, they will often mimic how they see you living that response. This can be disappointing, especially if you're not living according to biblical standards. They consider your example more important than words.

The good news is God has offered up some incredible resources to help line up our words with our actions. The result is improved character—in us and in our children.

Write God's Word on Your Heart Today

Character is more closely aligned with a long-term lifestyle than any well-developed, multi-step action plan. Character isn't something you can fake, and it improves the longer you follow God's "life plan." Let's check out how that works by looking at these important memory verses.

Endurance builds character,
which gives us a hope.
ROMANS 5:4 CEV

God blesses those people who refuse
evil advice and won't follow sinners
or join in sneering at God.
PSALM 1:1 CEV

Character means you may have to refuse the idea that you can live with a life segmented between a church service on the weekend and a self-directed life the rest of the week. Character means doing the right thing even when there may be no law against what you are doing. You will have to think of others first.

History is filled with stories of how men with strong character helped lead nations and, more importantly, their families. When you commit to developing strong character, you shouldn't be surprised when you see leadership qualities developing in you, and as a result, positively affecting your family.

Dear God, I'm not sure why it's easier to engage knee-jerk reactions than to plan my responses in advance. Help me see the need to live what I believe, and believe so strongly that my actions are rooted in obedience to You. Develop my character according to the plans you have for me. Amen.

Reputation

Choose a good reputation over great riches; being held in high esteem is better than silver or gold.
PROVERBS 22:1 NLT

My dad always told me that I would have plenty of work if I would show myself available, willing, and consistent. He was right. He has also been a lifelong example of what a good reputation looks like. I think he'd agree with Benjamin Franklin, "It takes many good deeds to build a good reputation, and only one bad one to lose it."

We've all seen the result of a bad deed that caused great destruction of what may have been a good reputation. The experience may have been personal, or you may have observed someone you care about who suffered the effects of a bad decision.

While it may take time, a good reputation can be reclaimed. Choosing to make good decisions may benefit your children and family more than anyone else. They need to see that by repenting (turning away) from poor choices and living to create, there is promise for better days ahead.

Write God's Word on Your Heart Today

If you've ever thought the notion of hiding God's Word in your heart seems strange, you're probably not alone. The idea is simply to embed God's Word deeply into your soul so that when you are faced with the decision to make wise or poor choices, you will be armed with healthy responses. This is why memorizing the following verses is important for building and maintaining a good reputation.

*Throw off your old sinful nature
and your former way of life,
which is corrupted by lust and deception.*
EPHESIANS 4:22 NLT

*Let everyone see that you are
considerate in all you do.
Remember, the Lord is coming soon.*
PHILIPPIANS 4:5 NLT

The value of reputation is a key ingredient in building character. Staying the course in the hard things will help deliver solid character and a good reputation.

The value you place on your reputation will either enhance or diminish the value your children place on its pursuit. We must invest in a good reputation, caring for it the way we would a valuable piece of art. This is the only way to ensure that our children will have a good example to follow.

Dear God, I admit there are days when it would be easy to give up. It would be simple to find my feet walking a path of least resistance. The mistakes I make in moments of weakness not only affect me, but affect my children and may cause people to look at my faith as something that is weak and ineffective. Walk with me each moment of this day and keep my feet on Your chosen path. Amen.

Good planning and hard work lead to prosperity,
but hasty shortcuts lead to poverty.
PROVERBS 21:5 NLT

We live on a big planet. We serve a big God. His desire is for us to view Him as our employer and provider. He gives us the ability to work, the air we breathe, the food we eat, the intellect to understand what needs to be done, and the principles that keep us moving toward Him.

David Livingstone was both a medical professional and a missionary. He took his skills to the heart of Africa when no one else would. He ventured into areas few had ever been. His motto was, "Fear God and work hard."

The fear of God means to hold God to the highest level of awe and gratitude. The work you do is not a means of salvation, but rather an acknowledgment that everything you have is His. This includes your ability to work. This perspective will leave a lasting impression on your children.

Write God's Word on Your Heart Today

It's short-sighted to view work as simply performing tasks that bring you closer to a weekend. You *should* enjoy your weekends and vacations, but work provides an opportunity to do something important with your time while keeping you from participating in activities that add nothing to your character or reputation. These memory verses will help us focus on how we should live.

Aspire to live quietly, and to mind your own affairs, and to work with your hands, as we instructed you, so that you may walk properly before outsiders and be dependent on no one.
1 THESSALONIANS 4:11–12 ESV

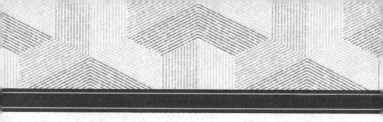

*Whatever you do in word or deed, do all in
the name of the Lord Jesus, giving thanks
through Him to God the Father.*
COLOSSIANS 3:17 NASB

The understanding of why we work and who we work for can create some great family dialogue. Show your children what it looks like to work hard, and then set some expectations that include their involvement. This is a solid life perspective that can benefit their own work ethic.

Dear God, even in those times when I am less than excited about work, help me to remember You have given me the skills to work and that when the end of the day arrives, it should be my goal to ensure that I have done my best for You. May others benefit from my work as I benefit from theirs. May my children learn the importance of working for You, too. Amen.

Reborn

Jesus replied, "Very truly I tell you, no one can see the kingdom of God unless they are born again."
JOHN 3:3 NIV

We are born selfish. We want what we want, and that usually means *now!* In time we come to believe that by our own ingenuity we can do life alone. Our hearts may open to a family, but the idea that we can get by on our own just never goes away.

Pride can pave the way as we walk before our children. They see the hard work, but they also see a hard shell. Amy Carmichael wisely said, "God, harden me against myself!" This is the place where we finally agree that God's plans for us are better than our own. We have all been given an invitation to become God's children, but our actions suggest we'd rather come to God on our own terms and without His help.

It can't be done.

Write God's Word on Your Heart Today

The goal of being transformed into something better than we are can't be accomplished without the "Transformer." No single self-help ideal will alter your eternity.

You are invited to be a man who, by example, shows your children what it looks like to accept God's gift of salvation, be transformed by the work of His Spirit, and grow into something much better than you ever were without Him. Are you ready to memorize the evidence?

*[Jesus said,] "You should not be surprised
at my saying, 'You must be born again.'"*
JOHN 3:7 NIV

Therefore, if anyone is in Christ, the new creation has come: The old has gone, the new is here!
2 Corinthians 5:17 NIV

To be reborn is to gain clarity in your thinking, receive forgiveness for your past, have peace in your present, and have hope in your future. It provides access to God's mercy, shows evidence of His grace, and offers guidance in every decision. If you accept this role of biblical manhood, the rest of this book will make more sense.

Dear God, I have wrestled with doing life alone. It hasn't worked. I understand the payment for life apart from You is death, and eternal life only comes when I submit to being reborn. You sent Your Son to pay the penalty for my sin and to bridge the gap so I could have the opportunity to come to You now. I believe. Teach me to follow. Amen.

Forgiven

There is therefore now no condemnation to those who are in Christ Jesus, who do not walk according to the flesh, but according to the Spirit.
ROMANS 8:1 NKJV

Forgiveness is a crucial aspect of being a father. We forgive our children because we've experienced God's forgiveness first-hand. Our kids will mess up because they come from a long line of humans who mess up. When we experience God's mercy we should be more willing to pass that mercy along.

All of us have a persistent voice that seeks to condemn us by saying, "You blew it." D. L. Moody puts this in perspective: "The voice of sin is loud, but the voice of forgiveness is louder."

When we agree with God that our "life mess" doesn't agree with God's plan for our lives, He shouts forgiveness into our souls.

God refuses to condemn His children, but He does want us to "own our stuff." If we've wronged God, we need to admit we are guilty and then accept God's forgiveness.

Write God's Word on Your Heart Today

Hymns are often used to teach truths about God. Charles Wesley explored the subject of sin and forgiveness when he wrote:

Depth of mercy! Can there be
Mercy still reserved for me?
Can my God His wrath forbear,
Me, the chief of sinners, spare?

I have long withstood His grace,
Long provoked Him to His face,
Would not hearken to His calls,
Grieved Him by a thousand falls.

Wesley's words suggest that he considered himself the worst of sinners. The hymn conveys the idea that he provoked God, didn't listen, and grieved Him through multiple failures. In this place where Wesley recognizes

30

his sin, he learns something equally important:

There for me the Savior stands,
Shows His wounds and spreads His hands.
God is love! I know, I feel;
Jesus weeps and loves me still.

That's the picture you should remember when memorizing the following:

If we confess our sins, He is faithful
and righteous to forgive us our sins
and to cleanse us from all unrighteousness.
1 JOHN 1:9 NASB

He was pierced for our rebellion, crushed for
our sins. He was beaten so we could be whole.
He was whipped so we could be healed.
ISAIAH 53:5 NLT

Dear God, I am grateful that in spite of my rebellion, You offer a way to forgive my sin. Help me to always be honest in agreeing that I fail. May Your mercy make me bold enough to forgive others. Amen.

Broken

My old self has been crucified with Christ.
It is no longer I who live, but Christ lives in me.
So I live in this earthly body by trusting in the Son
of God, who loved me and gave himself for me.
GALATIANS 2:20 NLT

Men are the protectors, providers, and caretakers of our families. We hate the idea of exposing our flaws. We like to view ourselves as veteran armor bearers with a liberal coating of invincibility. We envision ourselves as a blend of every action hero and old-time cowboy we have ever seen. We want others to view us as brave, fearless, and winners in everything we do.

Aesop is attributed with saying, "God will mend a broken heart if you give Him all the pieces," but most dads will entertain the idea that somehow we have to keep up appearances. We are flawed and imperfect, and deep down we struggle to admit we are insecure. When we admit to personal failure and brokenness, God can step in and do something with our imperfect lives.

Write God's Word on Your Heart Today

Is it less than manly to suggest that you allow your children to know your life is, or has been, broken? Is this opposed to the idea of building confident children? Your honesty with the struggles you face will allow your children to understand being broken is not only normal, but something that can be overcome. When we mask our struggle, it will be a challenge to show our kids God's redemption. Consider and memorize these incredible truths.

For the wages of sin is death, but the free gift of God is eternal life through Christ Jesus our Lord.
ROMANS 6:23 NLT

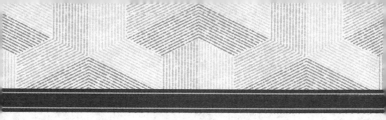

*If we claim we have not sinned, we make him out
to be a liar and his word is not in us.*
1 JOHN 1:10 NIV

If our children see us cover up our sinful behavior,
they will learn to cover up their mistakes as well.
Admitting our failings gives our children an up close and
personal experience with God's ability to repair broken
people.

*Dear God, it is so easy to put on masks.
I cover my brokenness believing I am making life
easier on my children. One day they will need to
seek Your restoration. I want them to remember
who their dad turned to when he was broken.
They can't remember what they have never seen.
Make me bold enough to admit brokenness. Amen.*

Transformed

So just as sin ruled over all people and brought them to death, now God's wonderful grace rules instead, giving us right standing with God and resulting in eternal life through Jesus Christ our Lord.
ROMANS 5:21 NLT

God calls dads to live radically reformed lives. He invites us to come to Him just like we are, but He never wants us to remain where we've been. To get a better understanding of this idea, think of someone who can't swim being rescued from deep water. Once safely in the boat, they jump over the side believing they suddenly know how to swim and wonder why their situation seems worse. Crazy, right?

When God starts to change us into who He made us to be, He asks for our cooperation. For God to change someone who is unwilling, refuses to be reshaped, and isn't convinced change in is their best interest may mean that God must work overtime to show us the wisdom of obedience.

Broken + New Life + Obedience = Transformation.

Write God's Word on Your Heart Today

Billy Sunday once said, "Churches don't need new members half so much as they need the old bunch made over."

We should never be so comfortable sitting in the audience at church that we become easily satisfied with staying away from the God who transforms. God desires so much more for your life. These memory verses demonstrate that.

I am certain that God, who began the good work within you, will continue his work until it is finally finished on the day when Christ Jesus returns.
PHILIPPIANS 1:6 NLT

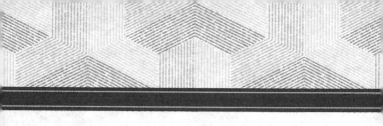

*I have been crucified with Christ and I no longer live,
but Christ lives in me. The life I now live in the body,
I live by faith in the Son of God, who loved me
and gave himself for me.*
GALATIANS 2:20 NIV

God provides salvation, offers a new life story, and
invites each of us to transformed living.

Adjusting and adapting to the new life God wants
can be a beautiful gift to our families. When children
observe our transformation they may be more inclined to
submit to their own life transformation.

Dear God, I am so glad You don't do a life makeover, but full-blown transformation. You turn a mean streak to kindness, retaliation to forgiveness, and hate to love. Help me cooperate in the change You are making. Let me never settle for a whitewashed life, because it's only pretend transformation. Amen.

Trust

The LORD is my strength and shield. I trust him with all my heart. He helps me, and my heart is filled with joy. I burst out in songs of thanksgiving.

PSALM 28:7 NLT

If you really want to teach your children to trust, you must show them what trust looks like. Actively trust the One who made you and promises a life plan specifically for you. Believing that He can lead and guide can go a long way in reducing the potential example of a jaded and suspicious life for your children.

When we look at the world around us, it's easy to pinpoint the things that fail to invite trust. Wisdom is knowing that trust is a value earned through consistent, faithful integrity.

There are many things we may not value enough to trust, but God knew you before you were born. Before your parents heard you cry, God already knew who you would be. Real men trust the "consistent, faithful integrity" of God and invite their children to join them.

Write God's Word on Your Heart Today

Not every person is worthy of your trust. Sometimes, it can feel difficult to believe that God is completely trustworthy. We think that if we really follow His life instructions we will somehow miss out on something better. Maybe this internal struggle is why we are repeatedly reminded to trust Him, and why scripture encourages us to share the news that trusting God leads to a full life.

Memorize the following passages as a reminder that trusting God is the best way to live. Internalize the message of these passages, and your worldview will change.

Those who know your name trust in you, for you, Lord, have never forsaken those who seek you.
PSALM 9:10 NIV

Trust in the LORD with all your heart, and lean not on your own understanding; In all your ways acknowledge Him, and He shall direct your paths.
PROVERBS 3:5–6 NKJV

When you are tempted to tackle every personal struggle on your own, decide to trust God's faithfulness instead. When you believe you're being denied something good, remember God's integrity prevents Him from doing anything less than the best for you.

Dear God, I would be lying if I said that I have never had trust issues with You. Maybe it's because I am unable to see everything You see, but I find myself hesitant to follow You when it's clear that You are leading me. When my children remember me in the future, I want them to recall a man who trusted God in the greatest adventure he knew—life. Help me be that man for them today. Amen.

If children, then heirs—heirs of God and joint heirs with Christ, if indeed we suffer with Him, that we may also be glorified together.
ROMANS 8:17 NKJV

When you're a dad, it might be difficult to think of yourself as a son, too. You might be a man whose father abandoned you. Your father might have left you a negative legacy. Your dad might have been amazing and have left you a legacy you think you could never live up to.

Rather than dwelling on a heritage you can't change, consider what *God* offers His children. You get life, salvation, forgiveness, hope, peace, and a future. When you are reborn into God's family you gain access to a legacy that follows you beyond death and will leave a lasting impression on your children and grandchildren.

Don't be defined by your past or by your father's past. It is your present choices that impact your future legacy. That legacy could inspire the choices of family members you have yet to meet.

Write God's Word on Your Heart Today

By accepting the invitation to become a child of God you are not only adopted into God's family, but are given access to every right, privilege, and responsibility of a child of God. You become a son of an amazing Dad. Need proof? Memorize these verses.

Some people accepted him and put their faith in him. So he gave them the right to be the children of God.
JOHN 1:12 CEV

God's Spirit makes us sure that we are his children.
ROMANS 8:16 CEV

Every truth that you memorize can help rescue you in times of temptation. There's no need to live through temptation or trials alone. God is with us through everything. . .nothing is too difficult for Him.

If you are a child of God, you can use what you read here as either a refresher course for who you are, or as a tool to help you discover a different life to which you've been called.

Dear God, as a son I've been disappointed by my father. As a father I've disappointed my chrildren. As I learn more about being Your child, and the many ways You're different from every other dad, I pray that what I learn helps me become a better son, and a better dad. You're the perfect example. Help me be a good son so, in turn,I can be a good dad. Amen.

Understand this, my dear brothers and sisters:
You must all be quick to listen, slow to speak,
and slow to get angry.
JAMES 1:19 NLT

It's been said that the reason we have two ears and one mouth is because we should listen twice as much as we speak.

We all know someone who refuses to listen to their children. They want to get a point across, so they lecture while their children's words are ignored. There are times when the child had no reasonable excuse for their actions, but the child quickly discovers their perspective has no value. As those kids grow they feel less comfortable sharing life with their father.

God asks us to come to Him even when we aren't happy with our circumstances. He doesn't limit His listening to when we are happy and obedient. He also listens when we are sad, angry, or in trouble. He desires to hear our hearts. He accepts our honest struggles. He *is* our example.

Write God's Word on Your Heart Today

The tradeoff for enjoying the benefit of the God who listens is that He wants us to return the favor. He wants us to listen and grow. He's an incredible teacher. He shares His thoughts through the Bible, and those principles are more than suggestions. Memorize and think on these ideas.

*Listen to counsel and accept discipline,
that you may be wise the rest of your days.*
PROVERBS 19:20 NASB

I will listen to what God the Lord says;
he promises peace to his people, his faithful
servants—but let them not turn to folly.
PSALM 85:8 NIV

It's frustrating when we think our children aren't listening. Is it so hard to believe that God says in His own way, "Hey, be quiet. Listen closely. What I have to say is important"?

Think about it. We have access to the greatest wisdom in the world. How often do we choose to attend seminars, read books, or watch a television show featuring wise people while ignoring a Bible filled with the ultimate wisdom?

Dear God, help me intentionally listen to You. I don't want to live on bite-sized wisdom snacks. I want to really hear what You have to say through Your Word. Then as I listen, help me take what I learn and listen to my own children. Help me use my two ears to listen more. Amen.

*Do to others whatever you would like them
to do to you. This is the essence of all that
is taught in the law and the prophets.*
MATTHEW 7:12 NLT

Have you noticed how easy it is to be rude?
Someone cuts us off in traffic and our thoughts turn
dark. Someone pushes their way ahead of us in a
checkout line, and we imagine they're a criminal.

Would it surprise you to learn that we should
expect injustice? Would it further surprise you to know
that when we receive injustice from someone, we're
called to be kind to them, to repay their evil with a
positive response?

Being kind means putting the needs, opinions,
and even the rudeness of others into perspective. They
might be rude, but we have to focus on our behavior,
not on theirs. Albert Schweitzer sums it up nicely:
"Constant kindness can accomplish much. As the sun
makes ice melt, kindness causes misunderstanding,
mistrust, and hostility to evaporate."

Write God's Word on Your Heart Today

We are often called to pay more attention to our actions and motives than to judge the rudeness of others. Integrity in relationships will often mean our actions won't rely on the choices of others. We should pre-decide how we will respond, and when we do that, we'll have a clearer understanding of how our kindness goes against our human nature.

When God's plan goes against what everyone else is doing—follow God. Etch these verses deep into the part of you that seeks to bring honor to God.

Never let loyalty and kindness leave you!
Tie them around your neck as a reminder.
Write them deep within your heart.
PROVERBS 3:3 NLT

Love is patient, love is kind. It does not envy,
it does not boast, it is not proud.
1 CORINTHIANS 13:4 NIV

Kindness always gives others more than they may deserve. Kindness enriches others and allows you to sleep well at night. Kindness is God using you to offer His best gifts to others.

*Dear God, kindness is not natural.
I learned very early in life that you get what
you deserve. The idea of being kind to people
who don't deserve it doesn't make sense to
me. But if You're the one asking me to be kind,
then I want to be brave enough respond in
a better way. I'll need Your help. Amen.*

*Let's not get tired of doing what is good.
At just the right time we will reap a harvest of
blessing if we don't give up.*
GALATIANS 6:9 NLT

Sometimes, I can't be patient under my own strength. I start strong, but it isn't long before I'm just moments away from exploding in front of the person that seems to be intent on frustrating me.

Just when I feel justified, Augustine adds perspective, "Patience is the companion of wisdom." So, if wisdom is what I seek, then a display of patience isn't about how inconvenienced I am, but how wisely invested I am in the lives of people God wants to touch. That includes people I meet every day, but also extends to my own children and family.

We persevere in patience because there's a positive end result coming, and in that knowledge we're left to remember that the reason God takes us through certain trials as dads is to shape godly character in the hearts of broken men.

Write God's Word on Your Heart Today

Think about individuals who've been positive influences in your life. Were they individuals who were easily frustrated and lacked patience? Or did they show a depth of care that left you feeling in awe of their longsuffering? The greatest influencers who have ever lived had characteristics that include patience, kindness, goodness, self-control, and integrity. Each of these attributes are common themes when describing wisdom.

When you're around these individuals, they can encourage you to be something more than you've been without making you feel like you're less than you are.

In the pursuit of patience we'll need to internalize and memorize a few things that lead to wisdom.

*Don't worry about anything; instead,
pray about everything. Tell God what you need,
and thank him for all he has done.*
PHILIPPIANS 4:6 NLT

*You know that the testing of your faith
produces perseverance.*
JAMES 1:3 NIV

The apostle Paul needed someone to encourage his spiritual growth. That someone was Barnabas, whose name meant, "Son of Encouragement." We all need a Barnabas in our lives, and we need to become a patient encourager for others.

*Dear God, I don't like to pray for patience
because I'm not sure I want to be patient.
I know this is something You want for me
because it reflects Your character. It dominates
the way You have dealt with me. If I'm to be
transformed into Your likeness, teach me to
accept patience as a mark of my commitment. Amen.*

Do not let kindness and truth leave you;
Bind them around your neck, Write them on
the tablet of your heart.
PROVERBS 3:3 NASB

Thomas à Kempis encourages, "Wait for the Lord.
Behave yourself manfully, and be of good courage.
Do not be faithless, but stay in your place and do not
turn back."

A journey with Jesus is not something to add to
an existing journey. It isn't to be a spiritual experiment
that can be discarded when something new comes
along. It *is*, in fact, a commitment to radical life
transformation. It's a commitment requiring faithful
backbone.

To turn your back on following Jesus is worse than
giving up on your favorite sports team or on a dream.
He made you, sustains you, and offers abundant life
to you. Lead so your children can follow.

We choose a life of faithfulness because Jesus
(our example) has never failed. Not once. His
faithfulness comes with the best guarantee our world
has ever seen. His faithfulness is forever.

Write God's Word on Your Heart Today

When my dad says something I usually remember it. I can't tell you the exact date he has said certain things, but I remember his advice. He said to leave things better than I found them and make myself available, consistent, and willing. Why do I remember? I value my relationship with my dad and view his words as important.

That's the idea behind memorizing the following verses. We internalize and practice what God says because we value our relationship and believe His words are important.

Be on the alert, stand firm in the faith,
act like men, be strong.
1 CORINTHIANS 16:13 NASB

*"If you are faithful in little things,
you will be faithful in large ones."*
LUKE 16:10 NLT

There's something special about getting advice from
God. He made the rules for righteous living. When we
dive into God's instruction manual we aren't really left
to grapple with what we are supposed to do. In fact,
Jesus summed the primary commands this way: "'You
must love the LORD your God with all your heart, all your
soul, and all your mind.' This is the first and greatest
commandment. A second is equally important: 'Love
your neighbor as yourself.'" (MATTHEW 22:37–39 NLT).

Dear God, You have been faithful to provide instructions for life. Your faithfulness includes love, forgiveness, peace, and salvation. I'm overwhelmed by the truth that even when I have been faithless, You kept Your promises. Thank You. Amen.

The truthful lip shall be established forever,
But a lying tongue is but for a moment.
PROVERBS 12:19 NKJV

Have you ever been guilty of selective honesty? You know, those times when telling a little white lie seems like a better idea than telling the truth? There are two problems with that. First, God says, "Don't do it." Second, when we lie, we can find ourselves in a place where we easily justify *every* dishonest action.

George Washington said, "I hope I shall possess firmness and virtue enough to maintain what I consider the most enviable of all titles, the character of an honest man."

An honest man can stand before the court and reveal facts without fear. An honest dad doesn't have to remember what he's told his children. For an honest man, trust is more easily offered, peace is easier to find, faithfulness is better understood, and best of all, forgiveness is more available. Honest truth combined with genuine love creates an atmosphere of transformation.

Write God's Word on Your Heart Today

Honesty about yourself is transparency. Honesty before God is humility. Honesty regarding God's truth is loving obedience.

Let the following two verses seep deep into your soul. Let them change any doubts you may have that honesty is God's policy. If we are committed to following God then these two memory verses point us in a powerful direction.

An honest witness can save your life,
but liars can't be trusted.
PROVERBS 14:25 CEV

Love does not delight in evil but rejoices with the truth.
1 CORINTHIANS 13:6 NIV

After spending time with these verses ask yourself, "How does a truthful witness save lives?" "Why does love rejoice with honesty?" "Have I made a habit of proclaiming lies?"

You need to be honest with yourself, your children, and with God. Honesty about decisions or actions can bring some negative consequences, but dealing with our inner dishonesty can bring ultimate healing, forgiveness, and restoration.

Dear God, Your Word tells me I sin.
I am reminded that I have been dishonest.
Even if I had the best intention, I understand this
character trait falls far short of Your best for me
and my interactions with my children, family,
and friends. May I make a conscious decision to
be honest in my dealings, honest in my failings,
and honest in my relationships. May I submit to
Your transformation with my entire life. Amen.

*Don't be selfish; don't try to impress others.
Be humble, thinking of others
as better than yourselves.*
PHILIPPIANS 2:3 NLT

It's safe to say that we live in a selfish time. Social media can alter our perspective of our self-worth. We can leave our computer feeling either better or worse about who we are. Chances are good that how we feel bears no resemblance to actual truth.

Taking a skewed mentality into everyday relationships can be dangerous. We make decisions on how we relate to others based on what we believe about ourselves. We can interact with others believing we are better than they are, or we think we're pathetic in comparison.

Since all of us deal with personal insecurities, we need an accurate view of who God thinks we are. If we are reborn, we are God's cherished children. Yet even in this exalted place we must intentionally choose to respect ourselves and others, refuse to be condescending to others, and care deeply for those around us.

Write God's Word on Your Heart Today

You've probably interacted with people who are intentionally respectful. . .people who value your opinions and who are a pleasure to be around. As a dad you have the opportunity to expect respect, but also to show it to your children. The idea of mutual respect is biblical. Commit the following to memory and let the words inform every aspect of your parenting and seep into every relationship you have.

Be devoted to one another in love.
Honor one another above yourselves.
ROMANS 12:10 NIV

Respect everyone, and love the family of believers.
1 Peter 2:17 NLT

If you aren't able to memorize these verses right now, no worries. . .they'll remain in your Bible. You can always go back and memorize them later. However, if you take these verses and hide them in your heart, you'll always have them available for immediate personal recall.

As followers of Jesus we have access to so much, but that access is never about what *we've* done, and all about what Jesus has freely given. Knowing this allows us to respect God and seek Him first in every area of our lives.

Dear God, You made me, You've accepted me, You're transforming me, and You're shaping my mind every day. Adjust my vision so I can see others the way You see them. May this change the way I respond to You. Amen.

Contentment

The fear of the LORD leads to life; then one rests content, untouched by trouble.
PROVERBS 19:23 NIV

Contentment. It's a place you find yourself when you're satisfied with your conditions. Contentment is a choice that allows you to find the good in the worst circumstances. It also allows you to humbly enjoy every good thing God provides. Charles Spurgeon wrote, "If you are not content with what you have, you would not be satisfied if it were doubled."

When other men get new toys, buy new houses, upgrade to a new car, or find a better neighborhood, we often wish we were like them. Envy steals contentment, which is why it should never be allowed as a house guest.

You will never be content with what you have if you're always dreaming of the next toy you want. Maybe that's why God sometimes withholds things we think we want. He's doing a work in our life that leads to contentment, and giving us everything we want detracts from that work.

Write God's Word on Your Heart Today

If your children seem unhappy with what they have, are demanding, and never satisfied, then it might be time to consider that they're following your bad example. When they see Dad unhappy with what he has, they imitate that and believe that the pursuit of bigger and better things is the best way to step into their future. Capture these memory verses, hide them deep, and let them affect your response, what you choose, and the things you pursue:

If we have food and clothing,
we will be content with that.
1 TIMOTHY 6:8 NIV

True godliness with contentment is itself great wealth.
1 TIMOTHY 6:6 NLT

Contentment differs from complacency. Complacency shows no interest in anything other than status quo. Complacency doesn't allow you to follow God because you are too comfortable where you are. Contentment is being willing to follow and accepting the conditions you actually face.

Dear God, I was born selfish. Being a father helps me see how selfish I can be, and how selfish my children can be. If I want my children to be content then they need to see that contentment in me. It's not easy when I see something I want, but can't afford. Can You help me learn? Give me the wisdom to respond in a way that rejects envy and selfishness and reflects the peace and contentment I find in knowing You have everything under control. Amen.

Grace

*He said to me, "My grace is sufficient for you,
for my power is made perfect in weakness."
Therefore I will boast all the more gladly about my
weaknesses, so that Christ's power may rest on me.*
2 CORINTHIANS 12:9 NIV

Imagine living in a country where there was only
one source of water. The natural spring located on
the land is owned by the king. Knowing the need for
fresh water, the great king issues a proclamation that
anyone who needed water could come to the palace
and take back as much as they need. There was
never a charge, and citizens would never be refused.

This is what grace looks like. Grace is having
access to something we could never get on our own.
In the case of our relationship to God, this is like
gaining access to a key that opens every door in His
kingdom. With grace we receive something we don't
deserve and could never buy.

We pray for daily grace because we are to ask
for what God has promised.

Write God's Word on Your Heart Today

When your child(ren) arrived you had only recently met them, but they were offered grace—the opportunity to have full access to everything you could provide. This included shelter, health care, love, respect, forgiveness, and gifts of time and protection.

Memorize the following verses and remember that when God gave the law, He knew we couldn't keep every single command. Receiving the truth of God's grace is only possible through the death, burial, and resurrection of Jesus. He paid the price for salvation, eternal life, forgiveness—and grace.

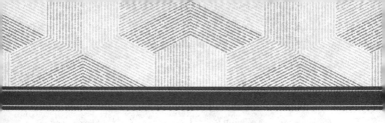

*For by grace you have been saved through faith;
and that not of yourselves, it is the gift of God;
not as a result of works, so that no one may boast.*
EPHESIANS 2:8–9 NASB

*For the law was given through Moses;
grace and truth came through Jesus Christ.*
JOHN 1:17 NIV

Once Jesus completed His work we were no longer
shackled to the law, but were freed by grace that
welcomed us into a relationship with God.

Dear God, why am I so easily persuaded that if I just do enough good things I can cancel any debt I might have with You?
You offered so much to me, but I struggle with accepting something I haven't worked for.
Your ways are so different, but You prove that when my perspective doesn't fit with Yours it should be abandoned. Help me see Your instructionsas pure, trustworthy guidance. Amen.

Give freely and become more wealthy; be stingy and lose everything. The generous will prosper; those who refresh others will themselves be refreshed.

PROVERBS 11:24–25 NLT

Did God create the earth? Did He create mankind?

If you said, "Yes," then you'll also understand that He created dirt, water, air, sunshine, and rain. He created minds to think with and compassion to share.

God provided everything we'd need. He then asks us to give to others. The giving that God asks of us is not only obedience, but to be an example. If our children see us as selfish there is an increased potential for a new generation of selfishness.

Charles Spurgeon sums things up, "It is beyond the realm of possibilities that one has the ability to out give God. Even if I give the whole of my worth to Him, He will find a way to give back to me much more than I gave."

Write God's Word on Your Heart Today

If our goal is to become more like Jesus then we will pursue generosity. Too often we look at what He provides as something we earn or something He gives that we can use for own purposes. The Bible is filled with examples of how God asks us to manage His resources. God desires to meet our genuine needs, but He wants to bless others through our hands. Maybe this has more to do with a plan to expand blessings rather than wallets.

"Give, and you will receive. Your gift will return to you in full—pressed down, shaken together to make room for more, running over, and poured into your lap."
LUKE 6:38 NLT

An evil person borrows and never pays back;
a good person is generous and never stops giving.
PSALM 37:21 CEV

Giving is a response of gratitude for God's outrageous generosity. God warns that the love of money makes it impossible to be a faithful manager of God's resources. Perhaps the best way to overcome this mindset is to understand at the core of our being that what we possess is a fully transferable gift that should always serve the purposes of a generous God.

*Dear God, help me manage Your provisions.
I can enjoy what You give, and share what
You lead me to share. If my heart and mind
must change, let the end result
be a generous heart. Amen.*

Joyful

I pray that God, the source of hope, will fill you completely with joy and peace because you trust in him. Then you will overflow with confident hope through the power of the Holy Spirit.

ROMANS 15:13 NLT

Joy comes from outside ourselves, it's the result of a spiritual gift. Maybe the reason we don't experience true joy before being reborn is so we'll recognize the inner longing for it when we see it in others.

Billy Sunday said, "If you have no joy, there's a leak in your Christianity somewhere."

It's easy to believe happiness and joy are the same thing, but happiness is an emotional response to experiences while joy is the knowledge that no matter what you face, God can be trusted with the outcome. This is why you can embrace joy even when going through the tough moments of life. Happiness will never let you do that.

Let joy remind you that you are no longer alone.

Write God's Word on Your Heart Today

Because there is confusion on the difference between joy and happiness, many will try to participate in as many fun and entertaining experiences as possible. However, when the experience is over they wonder why their feelings crash so easily. Help your children learn the difference. Too many children see amusement as a primary directive. Did you know God never promised happiness? Happiness is a poor substitute for joy. Why do we insist on settling for less?

Embrace God's gift of joy discovered in these verses.

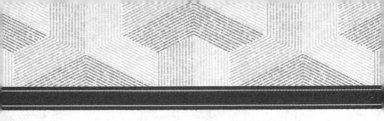

Be joyful in hope, patient in affliction, faithful in prayer.
ROMANS 12:12 NIV

Though you have not seen him, you love him; and even though you do not see him now, you believe in him and are filled with an inexpressible and glorious joy.
1 PETER 1:8 NIV

Savor life experiences, but don't expect those events to make a significant difference in your future. Joy never has to leave us.

Dear God, forgive me for the apathy I occasionally feel. It's easy for me to believe that if I'm not happy, something is wrong. Thanks for the reminder that joy is a more excellent pursuit. Allow me to access the joy You offer. Allow it to overflow and impact others. Allow it to improve my perspective. Amen.

Friendly

A friend is always loyal, and a brother is born to help in time of need.
PROVERBS 17:17 NLT

There's very little to compare to a great friend. David found one in Jonathan. Jesus found one in John. Some of us have one, but all of us need one. So, who does the heavy lifting to make friendship happen?

Albert Schweitzer said, "We cannot possibly let ourselves get frozen into regarding everyone we do not know as an absolute stranger."

Unconsciously we may believe that great friends will just appear one day. These new friends will accept our shortcomings, laugh at our jokes, and like the same things we like. This belief suggests we don't have to do anything but wait.

We can't expect others to simply meet our needs as friends without taking ownership of our responsibility for personal friendliness. We also can't become close friends with those who would come between us and a close relationship with God. They will make it too easy to turn away from the One who loves us.

Write God's Word on Your Heart Today

The two pillars of great friendships are:

1) Be a great friend.
2) Choose friendships carefully.

Read the verses below, and apply them to the friendships you have right now. Use them to find ways to *be* a better friend. Commit these verses to memory and share them with your family.

Do not be misled: "Bad company corrupts good character."
1 CORINTHIANS 15:33 NIV

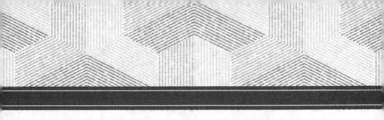

As iron sharpens iron, so one person sharpens another.
PROVERBS 27:17 NIV

Each reading in this book allows dads to
review a different character trait that can impact a
new generation. You may find this perspective isn't
remarkably different from your own, but it could be a
new concept. God wants to reshape our lives so that
we bear a greater resemblance to His Son, Jesus, in our
attitudes, actions, habits, interests, and obedience.

You could be the person God uses to help redefine
how your family lives life. Your children are growing up.
Are they seeing growth in you?

Dear God, beyond the desire to have You bring great friends into my life, I need You to help me be a great friend. Help me invest in relationships that strengthen my walk with You. May I become a better example of what that looks like so my children will always have an idea of how to be a better friend. Amen.

Follower

I want to know Christ and experience the mighty power that raised him from the dead. I want to suffer with him, sharing in his death, so that one way or another I will experience the resurrection from the dead!

PHILIPPIANS 3:10–11 NLT

Many men follow Christ as if they are viewing a spiritual do-it-yourself video. It's marginally fun to watch, provides some interesting information, and can be accessed whenever convenient. If we're true followers, then our goal is personal transformation—not Bible trivia.

Samuel Rutherford said, "I will believe and wait for Him, and will follow His providence, and not go before it, nor stay behind it."

Why is there such a strong comfort level in just sitting on the sidelines and believing that following is something we'll do *someday*? God is willing to guide us through each step we take. We are even given the Bible, which is the perfect "how-to" manual.

We only really demonstrate the importance of what we value by the conscientious commitment to following what we are passionate about.

Write God's Word on Your Heart Today

We follow people who follow God for fellowship and mutual encouragement. If you look to these people as the primary authority in how you live, then your focus shifts from the God you're supposed to follow to imperfect examples.

When you follow God you're committing yourself to learning more about Him, are obeying His commands, and are willing to leave your old way of living in favor of something new.

Meditate on, memorize, and follow the verses below.

Do not be conformed to this world, but be transformed by the renewal of your mind, that by testing you may discern what is the will of God, what is good and acceptable and perfect.
ROMANS 12:2 ESV

*Grow in the grace and knowledge of our Lord
and Savior Jesus Christ.*
2 PETER 3:18 NKJV

Each day brings the opportunity to choose whom we follow. We can wander a path we design, one suggested by another, or even a path we know won't end well. God's path is described as narrow and straight. We can also choose *this* path. Why is this path so easy to overlook?

Dear God, why is it that all the other paths seem so attractive? Help me understand that if I'm to be where You are then I need to go where You lead. May I choose to be willing to follow. Amen.

Disciple

Work hard so you can present yourself to God and receive his approval. Be a good worker, one who does not need to be ashamed and who correctly explains the word of truth.
2 Timothy 2:15 NLT

The difference between a follower and a disciple may be explained as the difference between earning a degree and agreeing to a post-graduate apprenticeship.

A disciple may be described as someone who has followed Jesus and has developed a passion for going deeper. They want to put into practice the things they are learning.

For the disciple there is always a price. G. K. Chesterton wrote, "Jesus promised the disciples three things—that they would be completely fearless, absurdly happy, and in constant trouble."

Discipleship is not an easy choice. Your passion will not be welcome by some who view your zeal as extreme. Your perspective will not match much of society. However, to move from follower to disciple is exactly what Jesus calls us to do.

Write God's Word on Your Heart Today

Do your children see godly passion in your home? Are they immersed in a home culture that promotes radical obedience?

When Jesus hand selected His disciples, He didn't choose just anyone. Sometimes He chose one who didn't even know who He was. Discipleship is a faith step that shouldn't be taken lightly. Not everyone is ready or even willing to be a disciple. While that may be true, God continues to prompt men just like you to grow, gain strength, embrace commitment, and join Him in the work He's been doing since the beginning of creation.

Let these memory verses steer you in the direction of discipleship.

"This is to my Father's glory, that you bear much fruit, showing yourselves to be my disciples."
JOHN 15:8 NIV

[Jesus said,] "Your love for one another will prove to the world that you are my disciples."
JOHN 13:35 NLT

Fruit and love. These are the two major descriptives in the above verses. We demonstrate growth by loving those who may be hard to love. That's not natural—that's discipleship.

Dear God, I'm not sure I will ever feel like a graduate of your discipleship school.
The idea of discipleship seems difficult, and it gets so uncomfortable. Since You call all Christians to be disciples, may I be willing to do what You ask with a passion that reflects the love You ask me to share. Amen.

*Let your good deeds shine out for all to see,
so that everyone will praise your heavenly Father.*
MATTHEW 5:16 NLT

When it comes to demonstrating Christ-like character, you might be in your first sprint. Or, you might be in a marathon. Wherever you find yourself, be the best example possible. These character traits and descriptions of godly daddyhood are not a "Guide to Perfect Parenting in Thirty-eight Easy Steps." Most of these chapters represent a work in progress. Since none of us have arrived at the place God calls us to, we have to set an example for each other. We won't be a perfect example, but we can always work toward improving.

D. L. Moody said, "Where one man reads the Bible, a hundred read you and me." What do others see?

The way you parent will likely be the way your children parent. How you view God will impact your child's perspective. The importance you place on a relationship with Jesus is an example your children need. Show what it looks like when God shows up in the life of the imperfect. Let your family see change as it happens.

Write God's Word on Your Heart Today

If we're going to be an example to our children, we must have an understanding of how to be an example. Since our goal is godly character, then we'll find perfect instructions in the Bible. Take time to embrace the following verses and then memorize them. You'll use these verses often to remind yourself that being an example is more than a suggestion.

Always set a good example for others.
Be sincere and serious when you teach.
Titus 2:7 CEV

Follow God's example, therefore,
as dearly loved children.
EPHESIANS 5:1 NIV

Being an example is a natural byproduct of being a follower and disciple. If you're really invested in seeking God with everything you've got, then others should begin noticing the difference between who you were and who you are becoming.

When people remember the old you, they should remember that person like they're reading an obituary. They remember who you were, but those memories no longer describe who you are. The old has gone. The new has come (see 2 Corinthians 5:17).

Dear God, when I think of being a godly example, my mind considers lots of different people. None of these people are me. How is it possible that You could take someone who must seek forgiveness on a regular basis and transform them into living examples of Your love, mercy, grace, and patience? If I'm to be an example, make me willing to follow. Amen.

Teacher

You must commit yourselves wholeheartedly to these commands that I am giving you today. Repeat them again and again to your children. Talk about them when you are at home and when you are on the road, when you are going to bed and when you are getting up.
DEUTERONOMY 6:6–7 NLT

Discipleship and teaching go together. We must move beyond a personal journey to something that impacts others. It's like moving from being a college graduate to becoming a professor. More than accumulating information, you're actively sharing how God took you from point A to point B. There is intentionality to everything you teach. There will be everyday moments where instruction takes place. There will be seasons when you'll carve out time to teach.

In our homes. . .a father's name should become synonymous with teaching. Not every child will learn what they need to know in a church youth group. If you want to ensure your children learn spiritual truth, you'll have to take the leadership role—and teach.

Write God's Word on Your Heart Today

Following God and being an example is a perfect life plan for dads. Consume and be consumed by God's Word. The passion for what you're learning will move you to become a teaching disciple. You may not feel you're ready, but by refusing to share truth, you're leaving your kids in the dark. God can use your mouth to speak His truth, but stick to what He has already said. If what you say contradicts the Bible, someone is wrong—and it's not God.

So why is it important to teach, and what are the tools? Memorizing these verses will answer those questions and remind you where to return for daily wisdom.

*All Scripture is God-breathed and is useful for teaching,
rebuking, correcting and training in righteousness.*
2 TIMOTHY 3:16 NIV

*Let the message about Christ completely fill your lives,
while you use all your wisdom to teach
and instruct each other.*
COLOSSIANS 3:16 CEV

God places a high calling on teaching. It's
something He asks each of us to take on. Embrace the
challenge.

Dear God, while the idea of teaching may not seem natural to me, I recognize it's something You ask of dads. May I never be so naïve as to believe my children will just "know" Your words. I had to learn, so do they. Give me courage, help me learn what I teach, and may I believe what You have written. Amen.

> *More than anything else, put God's work first and do what he wants. Then the other things will be yours as well.*
>
> MATTHEW 6:33 CEV

God tells us that we should plan, but He ultimately guides our way. That could lead a person to think that there is no real reason to plan anything. If God guides our steps, then it's pointless to plan. Right? We are also told that we are to seek God's will and follow it. Even that doesn't sound like there's much choice in the matter. So, why are we called to be planners?

Helen Keller, who was blind, once said, "The most pathetic person in the world is someone who has sight, but has no vision."

God wants to take His will and blend it with our passion. He wants us to identify with His direction and then use the skills and creative interests He's given us to move us to a place of both obedience and personal investment.

When we lack passion, we lack vision.

Write God's Word on Your Heart Today

Every plan we make should be drafted in sand, not cut in stone. God has ultimate veto power over our plans so be ready for change. Plans need to be thought of as subject to adjustment, adaptation, and complete alteration. Our part in planning is to simply be willing to move in the direction God leads and submit ourselves to His great adventure. When planning, keep these memory verses at the front of your mind.

Wherever your treasure is, there the desires of your heart will also be.
LUKE 12:34 NLT

He who follows righteousness and mercy finds life,
righteousness, and honor.
PROVERBS 21:21 NKJV

You have plans for your life. God has plans for your life. Seeing how well God did with things like air, food, and water, who do you think has the ability to make better plans? How amazing is it to think that God cares enough about you to have a plan and purpose that really invites you to use the passion and purpose that makes you unique.

Dear God, help me to find a comfort level between the plans I make and the plans You have for me. My vision of the future only considers what I know in this moment. Because You are all-knowing You can direct me in ways that are better than my best plans. Thanks for leading. Amen.

Obedient

*Loving God means keeping his commandments,
and his commandments are not burdensome.*
1 John 5:3 NLT

His name was Jake, and he was my mentor. From our first meeting there was little doubt he cared for people. Every new visit assured me he was an obedient teacher. He never gave me his opinion, except perhaps about college basketball.

When I would ask a question he would *always* say, "Let's see what God says." We'd look in scripture, and even when I wanted to debate with Jake, the point was not worth arguing. If it was in God's Word, then it was to be obeyed no matter what I might think.

Jonathan Edwards once wrote, "Resolution One: I will live for God. Resolution Two: If no one else does, I still will."

It can be easy to selectively adopt biblical truth. Many view biblical teaching as a spiritual buffet that you can adapt to match the way you already think. Any who try this method will bypass the benefits of life transformation.

Write God's Word on Your Heart Today

Obeying God shouldn't be viewed as a way to earn something. God loves us, and as our way of expressing gratitude for what He's already done, we obey. We must realize that His commands aren't intended to keep us away from what we consider fun, but to preserve our integrity for the future.

Memorize and identify with these verses. Catch sight of His faithfulness and choose obedience.

[Jesus said,] "If you love me, keep my commands."
JOHN 14:15 NIV

I have chosen to be faithful;
I have determined to live by your regulations.
PSALM 119:30 NLT

My friend Jake encouraged me to memorize God's Word and obey what I memorized. Find someone like Jake who will encourage your journey. At some point you may become someone like Jake. The need for godly examples is overwhelming. Prepare to pursue God long after you put this book down.

Dear God, it's difficult to obey. My world bends rules, seeks ways to find loopholes. Your Word is personal, and You ask for my obedience. If I refuse to obey, my example tells my children that Your rules don't apply to me—and they don't apply to them. Help me leave the excuses behind because if I refuse to obey I will never become the dad You want me to be. Amen.

Let the word of Christ dwell in you richly in all wisdom, teaching and admonishing one another in psalms and hymns and spiritual songs, singing with grace in your hearts to the Lord.

COLOSSIANS 3:16 NKJV

No one has to teach us how to be selfish. We seem to come by that perspective and attitude easily. Gratitude, on the other hand, takes practice.

A. J. Gossip once wrote, "Thanksgiving is the language of heaven, and we had better start to learn it if we are not to be mere dumb aliens there."

It's one thing to have a sense of gratitude, but another thing altogether to voice your appreciation. That's true for expressing gratitude to your friends, neighbors, children, and God.

Expressing meaningful gratitude to your children can go a long way toward maintaining good relationships and improving bad relationships. Show your children that you aren't selfish, and instead, that you're generous with gratitude.

Write God's Word on Your Heart Today

Gratitude is the recognition of a gift accepted. It's recognizing that someone thought enough to perform a task on your behalf. Gratitude is a personal response to the thoughtfulness of others.

Thankfulness is an attitude that invites community. When you're thankful, you're admitting that others have value. Perhaps God introduced the idea of gratitude to keep us from personal isolation.

The absolute best expressions of gratitude are the ones directed toward God. Why? He did everything needed to keep us from being isolated from Him. He offers salvation, forgiveness, and eternal life. Memorize the following and take some time to express gratitude.

*Give thanks in all circumstances; for this is God's
will for you in Christ Jesus.*
1 THESSALONIANS 5:18 NIV

*Enter his gates with thanksgiving; go into his courts with
praise. Give thanks to him and praise his name.*
PSALM 100:4 NLT

Make a list. Start with the things you are most
grateful for and then keep adding to the list. With every
item you place on your list you are more likely to feel
accepted, loved, and see others are more important than
you might have otherwise believed.

119

*Dear God, Your love for me should inspire
gratitude. Too often I find myself believing
I might be able to do enough "right" things
to earn Your approval on my own. Since I can't
save myself, the best response to Your love
is—gratitude. Thanks. Amen.*

Set Apart

You are a chosen people, a royal priesthood,
a holy nation, God's special possession, that you
may declare the praises of him who called you
out of darkness into his wonderful light.
1 PETER 2:9 NIV

Phillips Brooks said, "It does not take great men to do great things; it only takes consecrated men."

The word *consecrated* is rarely used these days, but it means to be dedicated, holy, and set apart. That's how God sees those who are reborn and transformed. We become something very useful when we're set apart for a work God has created us to do.

You might have some china that once belonged to your grandma. These place settings are only used on special occasions. They are set apart for a particular use.

To be a dad set apart for God to use doesn't mean you're seldom used, but rather strategically used in specific situations. You have been given particular skills God will use, with your cooperation, to affect change in your family, neighborhood, and world.

Write God's Word on Your Heart Today

When we find ourselves living comfortably in a life that doesn't value God's commands, we're too comfortable to be "set apart." Life is too good, and we're too happy to do the uncomfortable thing of following God.

At least one Bible translation refers to those who are set aside as "peculiar people." Peculiar simply means "different." As God's disciples, we're called to live differently, not as the world lives.

Memorize the following, and let God set you aside for His work while He sets you up for success—His way.

*You can be sure of this: The LORD set apart
the godly for himself.*
PSALM 4:3 NLT

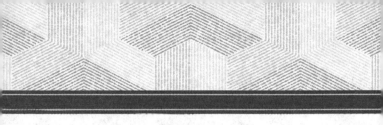

If you keep yourself pure, you will be a special utensil for honorable use. Your life will be clean, and you will be ready for the Master to use you for every good work.
2 Timothy 2:21 NLT

Christians have been described as God's hands and feet. We go where He sends, and we do what He instructs. When transformation takes place in our lives, we're more willing to embrace a servant's heart that God develops in those He sets apart.

Dear God, there's something exciting about knowing You have a special purpose for me. I'm honored that my life could be used to impact others on Your behalf. There's also some fear I won't be willing when the time comes, or I will fail to understand what You want from me. Make my heart responsive enough that when You call I will easily understand the need to follow. Amen.

Honorable

*Finally, brethren, whatever things are true,
whatever things are noble, whatever things are just,
whatever things are pure, whatever things are lovely,
whatever things are of good report, if there is any
virtue and if there is anything praiseworthy—meditate
on these things. The things which you learned and
received and heard and saw in me, these do,
and the God of peace will be with you.*

PHILIPPIANS 4:8–9 NKJV

More than 400 years ago Christopher Marlowe wrote, "Virtue is the fount whence honour springs."

God instructs us to be honorable in our conduct. We become honorable when we take God's commands and make them central to our conduct. Not just when people watch us, but all the time. We're also to align ourselves with those things we know to be honorable. Interestingly, we are to *be* honorable and *act* honorably without demanding that others *acknowledge* our actions.

In turn, we offer honor and glory to God daily because of the incredible way He's given us all things to enjoy.

Be honorable and give honor back to God.

Write God's Word on Your Heart Today

When you invest time in memorizing verses that connect with being honorable, you'll discover there's a step you take before ever getting to the "honorable" stage. That step is humility. When replacing self-esteem with self-respect we become more humble and increasingly more honorable. Why? If you thought self-esteem and self-respect were the same, you should know that the first deals with making us feel better about ourselves in all situations. The second values making the right choices no matter how it makes you feel. That kind of discipline earns honor.

Wisdom's instruction is to fear the LORD,
and humility comes before honor.
PROVERBS 15:33 NIV

Never pay back evil with more evil. Do things in such a way that everyone can see you are honorable.
ROMANS 12:17 NLT

Humility always precedes honor. We then place that honor in the hands of God. He gave the skills while offering the choice to affect our world with His love and truth. Why? As my son said after receiving a student-of-the-month award, "Why get too excited about an award for doing my best? I just did what you asked of me." Profound words.

Dear God, teach me what it means to be humbly honorable. Help me find affirmation in the honor, but pleasure in "passing on" the honor and glory to the One who is making me so much better than I've ever been on my own. Amen.

Make every effort to add to your faith goodness; and to goodness, knowledge; and to knowledge, self-control; and to self-control, perseverance; and to perseverance, godliness.
2 PETER 1:5–6 NIV

One of the hardest things for humans to master is self-discipline. This means telling yourself no to some things you'd really like to do, have, or try. It also means looking at life's big picture and embracing delayed gratification. While it may be true that good things come to those who wait, it doesn't mean the waiting is easy.

The same is true of our conscience. Austin Phelps wrote, "A disciplined conscience is a man's best friend. It may not be his most amiable, but it is his most faithful monitor."

Our conscience indicates when we aren't living a disciplined life. The self-control indicator could be used in determining what you eat, how much you work out, what you say, the places you will and will not go, what you read, and the time you will spend learning how to live like a Christian.

Write God's Word on Your Heart Today

What areas of self-discipline do you struggle with most?
We all wrestle with telling ourselves no.

What's the opposite of self-discipline? If you said
self-indulgence you might be in the majority. There's
a struggle between God's grace and self-indulgence.
When we indulge, we need God's grace. God *does*
provide grace (that's His part), but we're to exercise self-
control so that we don't take God's grace for granted.

Memorize these verses and consider how your
cooperation impacts change.

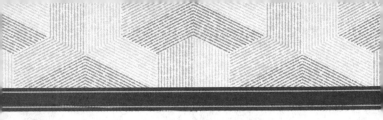

*A person without self-control is like a city
with broken-down walls.*
PROVERBS 25:28 NLT

*Be alert and of sober mind. Your enemy the devil
prowls around like a roaring lion looking
for someone to devour.*
1 PETER 5:8 NIV

Even in self-discipline God offers assistance. Ask for
His help and seek His wisdom.

Dear God, practicing self-control is like trying a new diet or buying a membership to a gym. It sounds good until it comes time to do it. Choosing to discipline myself makes me confront selfishness, entitlement issues, and the fact that I just don't want to resist what I like to do most. I need Your help to see the wisdom of pursuing Your plan for me. Amen.

Wise

Look carefully then how you walk, not as unwise but as wise, making the best use of the time, because the days are evil. Therefore do not be foolish, but understand what the will of the Lord is.
EPHESIANS 5:15–17 ESV

Have you ever met a person who attended college, but doesn't seem very wise? Have you ever met someone who never went to school, but seems to breathe wisdom? There's got to be a reason for this contradiction. Charles Spurgeon explains, "Wisdom is the right use of knowledge. To know is not to be wise. Many men know a great deal, and are all the greater fools for it. There is no fool so great a fool as a knowing fool. But to know how to use knowledge is to have wisdom."

For the dad who seeks to be transformed, the wisdom for transformation comes from God. Taking what we read, asking God's Spirit for help in understanding, and applying what's learned to the journey are all part of the journey toward godly wisdom.

Write God's Word on Your Heart Today

For an individual who loves facts and holds on to multiple bits of trivia, we use the term "brain glob" to describe the glut of knowledge the person is holding in their head. This can be useful if your goal is to win trivia games or prepare for a game show, but it's not *exactly* wisdom.

Ask God for wisdom. He won't make you memorize sports statistics, recent news about celebrities, or remember the name of every song you've heard. Why? He asks us to learn the Bible, which is the place where God's wisdom is written. The Bible contains wisdom that prepares you for eternity instead of tomorrow's water cooler conversation. Memorize these verses and pursue wisdom.

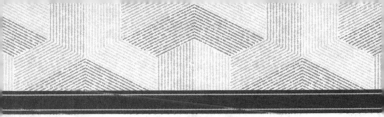

*If any of you need wisdom, you should ask God,
and it will be given to you. God is generous
and won't correct you for asking.*
JAMES 1:5 CEV

*A fool finds pleasure in wicked schemes, but a person
of understanding delights in wisdom.*
PROVERBS 10:23 NIV

It's encouraging to know God intends for us to be wise. He wants us to investigate His commands and promises. He wants us to understand how to respond to His correction. He wants us to take our understanding and use it to encourage others to gain wisdom.

Dear God, I want to prioritize the things that are important to learn. Help me pay more attention to You and less to every other bit of knowledge. Let me use what I know to build into the lives of my children. Amen.

Loving

Dear friends, let us love one another,
for love comes from God. Everyone who loves
has been born of God and knows God.
1 John 4:7 NIV

If we don't understand the love of God, then we may demand that those we say we love show constant proof of their love. We frequently view love as something ruled by justice and equality. This shows up in phrases like, "I love you when. . ." or "I'll love you if. . .". We put conditions on our love. This is dangerous in parenting. We are called to love—no matter what.

God never asks for equality in love. We are told in the Bible the only reason we can love is because He loved us first. (See 1 John 4:19.) It may be reasonable to say that the purest form of love is only achieved as we develop our relationship with God. Fyodor Dostoevsky said, "To love someone means to see him as God intended him."

Accept God's love and reflect what you've accepted.

Write God's Word on Your Heart Today

1 Corinthians 13 is known as the love chapter and is a great resource to show us what real love is. Love is patient, kind, never gives up, never loses faith, and is both hopeful and enduring. That's a great start, but there's also a list of things that do not show love. These include jealousy, boastfulness, pride, rudeness, demands, irritability, rejoicing in injustice, and keeping track of every wrong.

There is one more key to love that may alter your perspective. Love is a choice. We intentionally choose to love. Feelings can be a great bonus, but never a valid indicator of love. This is as true for our spouse as it is for our children.

Memorize these verses and find ways to demonstrate to your children what you've learned.

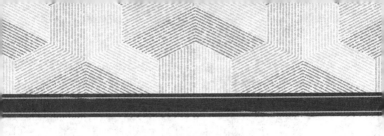

Let all that you do be done in love.
1 CORINTHIANS 16:14 NASB

I am giving you a new commandment: Love each other.
Just as I have loved you, you should love each other.
JOHN 13:34 NLT

You may remember Jesus gave two great
commandments—love God and then love everybody else.

Dear God, it's easy to view love as performance based. It's easy to withhold love. You give Your love without condition, and that's how You want me to love. Help me demonstrate that choice today. Amen.

Imperfect

For it is by grace you have been saved, through faith—and this is not from yourselves, it is the gift of God—not by works, so that no one can boast.
EPHESIANS 2:8–9 NIV

Every reading in this book deals with qualities dads should embrace. Why add a chapter about being imperfect? The reason has everything to do with peeling back our personal mask to reveal what we all know, but find hard to admit: We're imperfect.

Until we understand and acknowledge we have always lived below God's standards, we'll struggle with our relationship with God. Augustine wrote, "It is the function of perfection to make one know one's imperfection."

None of us deserve God's favor. We can't come close to His perfection. However, everyone can come to Him and accept His grace, salvation, and love. It's foolish to boast about our goodness because, next to God, our personal virtue falls short.

Because we're imperfect—God loved us enough to redeem us.

Write God's Word on Your Heart Today

Imperfection follows us through every aspect of life. When we get behind the wheel, when we try to be an example to our children, when we're at work, and even when we're all alone. It can be easy to put on a mask and hope no one will notice or get depressed because we think we should be better than that. Remember, you were born human, and humans are imperfect. Memorize these verses for a better understanding of what you bring to God and what He offers to you.

All have sinned and fall short of the glory of God.
ROMANS 3:23 NKJV

*God showed his great love for us by sending Christ
to die for us while we were still sinners.*
ROMANS 5:8 NLT

If perfection was possible for us, we wouldn't need
God's transformation. The old hymn, "Just As I Am,"
describes someone who doesn't try to clean themselves
up before coming to Jesus. This is the picture we need of
imperfection. On our own we can never clean ourselves
up enough. God knows who we are. He's willing to
change who we've been.

Dear God, sometimes it's easier to pretend perfection than admit mistakes. I can mentally beat myself up for my flaws and wonder how You can accept me. I fall short. I sin. Still, You love me. I will never be perfect, but I can be transformed. Let me start with obedience. Amen.

*Therefore, put on every piece of God's armor so you
will be able to resist the enemy in the time of evil.
Then after the battle you will still be standing firm.*
EPHESIANS 6:13 NLT

It is not a contradiction to say that imperfect dads
should also be full-time warriors. When we admit
our weaknesses, we gain His strength. Henry Ward
Beecher said, "The strength of a man consists in
finding out the way in which God is going, and
going in that way, too."

God never intends for us to stay weak. He wants
us to get up, use His armor, and be intentional about
standing firm.

Discovering and admitting weaknesses may
be a bit like boot camp. We may feel broken,
disappointed in ourselves, and wonder if we could
ever be used by God. However, God follows up
this period of brokenness and calls us to accept His
forgiveness.

Get ready for adventure. Stand up, suit up, and
look up. He's got a plan—and He's calling your
name.

Write God's Word on Your Heart Today

The New Testament idea of being a spiritual warrior refers to resisting evil influence. The armor of God (See Ephesians 6) describes equipment that can ward off an enemy. We stand our ground and resist our adversary. We don't do this for personal glory, but in obedience to the One who commands us to stand firm. We benefit, our families benefit, and the light of God's holiness shines brighter for all to see. Memorize these two verses and discover the patience, self-disciple, and character of a godly warrior.

Finally, be strong in the Lord and in the strength of his might.
EPHESIANS 6:10 ESV

Be strong, and let your heart take courage,
all you who wait for the LORD!
PSALM 31:24 ESV

God's warriors are called to resist, not attack. This is an important distinction. When we attack others in the name of our faith we can no longer demonstrate one of Jesus' two great commandments—love others. We stand firm resisting evil influence in our homes. We stand strong in a faith that is vibrant, life changing, and eternal.

Dear God, because I'm imperfect, help me to accept Your armor as a means of setting myself apart. Let me resist those things that bring no spiritual health to my family. May I learn to appreciate every piece of the armor You provide for my benefit and protection. Help me to stand firm today. Amen.

Athlete

Anyone who competes as an athlete does not receive the victor's crown except by competing according to the rules.

2 TIMOTHY 2:5 NIV

There are many connections between a Christian and an athlete. Like a marathon runner, we endure for longer than we may feel possible. We push harder than we want to push. Fatigue fills our thinking and impedes our progress. We don't just compete, we endure. We don't just endure, we persevere. Oswald Chambers wrote, "Perseverance is more than endurance. It is endurance combined with absolute assurance and certainty that what we are looking for is going to happen."

The apostle Paul could run his race because he had a certainty that the end would justify the difficulties he faced. This is the challenge for the warrior athlete; keep running knowing something better waits at the finish line that will make a little suffering now seem nothing more than a slight irritation.

Run, endure, and persevere. God is faithful. It will be worth it.

Write God's Word on Your Heart Today

Being a spiritual athlete has nothing to do with shoes, breathing techniques, or proper hydration. The finish line is eternal life with God. Our spiritual athleticism hinges on cooperation with God's commands. We should be faithful in difficult circumstances. Figuratively speaking, we run, we endure, and we persevere. We run in a way that that allows us to recall the best parts of the race, not a laundry list of life regrets. Memorize the verses below, and run well.

I have fought well. I have finished the race,
and I have been faithful.
2 TIMOTHY 4:7 CEV

*I discipline my body like an athlete, training it to do
what it should. Otherwise, I fear that after preaching to
others I myself might be disqualified.*
1 CORINTHIANS 9:27 NLT

All runners need a coach who encourages race
engagement leading to victory. We don't run alone,
but we also don't run against others. It's not a race to
see who's first, but who's faithful. It's not a race to gain
salvation, it is a race to prepare for heaven.

Dear God, there are times to rest, and I need them. Too often it's easier for me to watch others run because life seems too hard. Even if my race looks like walking, help me take those steps. Help me see the finish line. Help me endure and persevere in faithfulness and with intentionality. Thanks for being with me every step of my journey. Amen.

Ambassador

I have told all your people about your justice.
I have not been afraid to speak out, as you,
O LORD, well know.
PSALM 40:9 NLT

When someone is selected to be an ambassador, they become a representative who takes the policies of his country and uses them to influence, inform, and invite others to see the perspective of a foreign power. Christian dads have the same opportunity. You can be a godly ambassador and help your children have a better understanding of God's policies that can alter perspectives.

If it seems difficult to consider the task of an ambassador, you should consider the benefits package. Consider what George MacDonald wrote, "This is a sane, wholesome, practical, working faith: That it is a man's business to do the will of God; second, that God himself takes on the care of that man; and third, that therefore that man ought never to be afraid of anything."

An ambassador who follows the will of God can fulfill his role without fear and with profound joy.

Write God's Word on Your Heart Today

Ambassadors speak on behalf of another. They represent a culture, an ideal, and a hope. The result of an ambassador's work is found in a better understanding of God and an improved interest in learning more. Ambassadors bridge the gap between cultures. Memorize these verses for practical ways to demonstrate how God sees you as ambassador.

Whatever you do or say, do it as a representative of the Lord Jesus.
COLOSSIANS 3:17 NLT

*We are ambassadors for Christ, as though God
were pleading through us: we implore you
on Christ's behalf, be reconciled to God.*
2 Corinthians 5:20 NKJV

If a respected leader asked you to deliver a message, would you view this as a task or an honor? God's message changes futures, and He wants you to share. Will you treat this task lightly, or will it lead to an honorable example? There's a significant weight associated with being an ambassador. You represent something much larger than yourself. Don't treat the task lightly.

Dear God, I am honored that You want me to be an ambassador. May I take the time to learn more about You so I can help others understand the culture of life You offer. Take my failings and continue to transform my heart. I am imperfect, and my life may not reflect Your best, but take what little I have and make it useable for Your purpose and plan. Amen.

Dad

You yourself must be an example to them by doing good works of every kind. Let everything you do reflect the integrity and seriousness of your teaching.
TITUS 2:7 NLT

It just seems right for us to finish our time together understanding and celebrating the role of fathers in the lives of their children. The task you have as a dad may be more important than you realize. George Herbert said, "One father is more than a hundred schoolmasters."

Everything God is building into your life should be the things you pass along to your children. To learn something that changes your life and refuse to pass it on is a dishonor to the work God is doing. Be the follower who becomes a disciple. Be the example that is the mark of an ambassador. Be the obedient man that undergoes transformation.

Your children need you to be more than a good provider and chauffeur. They're looking to follow your example. Children often want to walk in your footsteps. Where are your steps leading?

Write God's Word on Your Heart Today

Our sons watch us shave and want to do the same. Our daughters see what makes us smile and try to make us laugh. Children will hide and want to be found. They will get mad and hope you will help them get over the anger. You are a super-hero. You're stronger, smarter, and better-looking than any other dad. The things you value become the things they consider valuable. They need guidance, and these memory verses help demonstrate the need to embrace the role of fatherhood.

Direct your children onto the right path, and when they are older, they will not leave it.
PROVERBS 22:6 NLT

*Fathers, do not provoke your children to anger, but bring
them up in the discipline and instruction of the Lord.*
EPHESIANS 6:4 ESV

You are more than a buddy. You hold the hearts of
children (no matter their age), and they want to trust you.

Review these pages for encouragement. Regularly
explore the Bible for best results.

Dear God, I love being a dad. Let me be the protector, defender, leader, and forgiven follower my children need. Lead me to the plans You've made for me, and let me willingly accept Your best. Equip me for every next day I get to spend with my children. May they see You in me. Amen.

Scripture Index

About the Author

Glenn Hascall is an accomplished writer with credits in more than fifty books, including titles from Thomas Nelson, Bethany House, and Regal. His articles have appeared in numerous publications including the *Wall Street Journal*. He's also an award-winning broadcaster, lending his voice to national radio and television networks.